Desserts
RECIPE SAMPLER

From the
AMISH-COUNTRY
COOKBOOK
Series

EVANGEL PUBLISHING HOUSE
NAPPANEE, INDIANA

DESSERTS Recipe Sampler

Copyright © 2000 by Evangel Publishing House. All rights reserved. No part of this book may be reproduced or transmitted in any form or by any means, electronic or mechanical, including photocopying, recording, or by any information storage and retrieval system, without permission in writing from the Publisher.

Evangel Publishing House
2000 Evangel Way, P.O. Box 189
Nappanee, IN 46550
Toll-free Order line: (800) 253-9315
Web-site: www.evangelpublishing.com

ISBN: 1-928915-09-4

Printed in the United States of America

10 9 8 7 6 5 4 3 2 1

Bob and Sue Miller grew up in a small Amish community in Sugarcreek, Ohio. Christian teaching and good home cooking were part of their upbringing, a heritage which continued when they established their own home. In 1971, the Millers opened Das Dutchman Essenhaus, a six-day Amish restaurant in Middlebury, Indiana, complete with Amish and Mennonite cooks and wait-staff.

After enjoying a memorable dining experience, many guests asked about the unique recipes prepared in the Essenhaus kitchens. The Millers responded with a set of three cookbooks containing their own original recipes and others gathered from their employees.

The resulting three-volume series of ***AMISH-COUNTRY COOKBOOKS*** has sold more than 500,000 copies since Volume 1 was introduced in 1979. In 2000, six "sampler" mini-cookbooks were created, using recipes chosen from the larger three-volume set:

- ***Snacks & Appetizers***
- ***Breads & Soups***
- ***Salads & Vegetables***
- ***Main Dishes***
- ***Cookies***
- ***Desserts***

To order additional "sampler" mini-cookbooks or the full-size ***AMISH-COUNTRY COOKBOOKS***, contact your local bookstore or gift store. Or you may contact Evangel Publishing House directly. An order form is enclosed at the back of this book.

CONTENTS

CAKES

Apple Butter Cake 1
Bundt Cake 2
Chocolate Angel Food Cake 3
Chocolate Zucchini Cake . . 4
Cream-Filled Sponge Cake . 5
Creme de Menthe Cake 6
Crumb Cake 7
Delicious Coffee Cake 8
Delicious Raspberry Cake . . 9
Easy Carrot Cake 10
Fresh Apple Cake 11
Happy Valley Chocolate
   Cake 12
Hot Fudge Sundae Cake . . . 13
Oatmeal Chocolate Chip
   Cake 14
Peach Custard Cake 15
Rhubarb Cake 16
Sour Cream Coffee Cake . . . 17
Turtle Cake 18

PIES

Angel Food Pie 19
Blueberry Lemon Pie 20
Bob Andy Pie 21
Coconut Cream Pie 22
Cream Cheese Pecan Pie . . . 23
Dutch Apple Pie 24
Fudge Sundae Pie 25
Fruit Pie with 7-Up 26
Green Tomato Pie 27
Lemon Cake Pie 28
Paradise Pumpkin Pie 29
Peach Cream Pie 30
Peanut Butter Pie 31
Raspberry Cream Pie 32
Rhubarb Custard Pie 33
Shoofly Pie 34
Strawberry Pie 35
Velvety Custard Pie 36
Never Fail Pie Crust 37
Short Cut Pastry 38

OTHER DESSERTS

Baked Rhubarb Crunch . . . 39
Bread Pudding 40
Cinnamon Pudding 41
Dirt Pudding 42
Death by Chocolate 43
Frozen Mocha Cheesecake . . 44
Fruit Pizza 45
Grandma Clark's
   Rice Pudding 46
Heath Bar Delight 47
Homemade Ice Cream . . . 48
Individual Cheesecakes 49
Old Fashioned Apple
   Dumplings 50
Peach-A-Berry Cobbler 51
Peanut Delight 52
Pretzel Dessert 53
Pumpkin Roll 54
Raspberry Freeze 55
Strawberry Cheesecake
   Trifle 56

Index to Recipe Location in the AMISH-COUNTRY COOKBOOK Series

Recipe Name   Vol. No.; Page No.

CAKES
Apple Butter . . . . Vol. 1, 111
Bundt . . . . Vol. 1, 114
Choc. Angel Food . . Vol. 3, 201
Choc. Zucchini . . . . . Vol. 3, 201
Crm-Filled Sponge . Vol. 2, 124
Creme de Menthe . . Vol. 3, 204
Crumb . . . . Vol. 1, 124
Delicious Coffee . . . . Vol. 3, 205
Delicious Rasp. . . . . . Vol. 2, 125
Easy Carrot . . . . Vol. 3, 207
Fresh Apple . . . . Vol. 1, 109
Happy Valley Choc. . Vol. 1, 118
Hot Fudge Sundae . . Vol. 1, 127
Oatmeal Choc. Ch. . . Vol. 2, 132
Peach Custard . . . . . Vol. 2, 134
Rhubarb . . . . Vol. 1, 136
Sour Cream Coffee . . Vol. 3, 215
Turtle . . . . Vol. 2, 141

PIES
Angel Food . . . . Vol. 1, 199
Blueberry Lemon . . . Vol. 3, 222
Bob Andy . . . . Vol. 1, 202
Coconut Cream . . . . Vol. 3, 226
Cream Ch. Pecan . . . Vol. 2, 202
Dutch Apple . . . . Vol. 1, 200
Fruit with 7-Up . . . . Vol. 2, 205
Fudge Sundae . . . . . . Vol. 3, 230
Green Tomato Pie . . Vol. 3, 114
Lemon Cake . . . . Vol. 3, 232
Never-Fail Crust . . . . Vol. 2, 193
Paradise Pumpkin . . Vol. 2, 213
Peach Cream . . . . . . Vol. 3, 234
Peanut Butter . . . . . . Vol. 2, 214
Raspberry Cream . . . Vol. 2, 218
Rhubarb Custard . . . Vol. 1, 222
Shoofly . . . . Vol. 1, 223
Shortcut Pastry . . . . . Vol. 1, 198
Strawberry . . . . Vol. 1, 224
Velvety Custard . . . . Vol. 1, 210

OTHER DESSERTS
Bread Pudding . . . . . Vol. 2, 227
Cinnamon Pudding . Vol. 1, 241
Death by Choc. . . . . . Vol. 3, 258
Dirt Pudding . . . . Vol. 3, 259
Fr. Mocha Ch. Cake . Vol. 2, 239
Fruit Pizza . . . . Vol. 2, 237
Heath Bar Delight . . Vol. 1, 248
Ice Cream . . . . Vol. 3, 277
Ind. Cheesecakes . . . Vol. 2, 124
Old Fashioned Apple
   Dumplings . . . . Vol. 1, 233
Peach-a-Berry Cob. . . Vol. 1, 253
Peanut Delight . . . . . Vol. 2, 246
Pretzel Dessert . . . . . Vol. 3, 269
Pumpkin Roll . . . . . . Vol. 1, 255
Raspberry Freeze . . . Vol. 2, 251
Rhubarb Crunch . . . Vol. 2, 230
Rice Pudding . . . . . . Vol. 3, 261
Straw. Cheese Trifle . Vol. 3, 275

Apple Butter Cake

1/2 cup shortening
1 cup sugar
4 eggs, beaten
2 1/2 cups flour
1 1/2 tsp. baking soda
1/2 tsp. salt
1 tsp. cinnamon
1/2 tsp. cloves
1/2 tsp. nutmeg
1 cup sour milk or buttermilk
1 cup apple butter

Beat together shortening and sugar; add eggs. Sift together dry ingredients. Add to the egg mixture alternately with milk. Mix in apple butter.
Bake in a greased loaf pan at 325° for 40 minutes or until done.

Meda Bontrager, waitress

Strawberry Cheesecake Trifle

- 2 - 8 oz. pkgs. cream cheese
- 2 cups powdered sugar
- 1 cup dairy sour cream
- 1/2 tsp. vanilla
- 1/4 tsp. almond flavoring
- 1 cup whipping cream
- 1/2 tsp. vanilla
- 1 tbsp. sugar
- 1 angel food cake, torn into bite-size pieces
- 2 quarts fresh strawberries, thinly sliced
- 3 tbsp. sugar
- 3 tbsp. almond flavoring

In a large bowl, cream together cream cheese and powdered sugar. Add sour cream, vanilla, and almond flavoring. Set aside. In a small bowl, mix whipping cream, vanilla, and sugar. Fold whipped cream into cream cheese mixture. Add cake pieces. Set aside.

Combine strawberries, sugar, and almond flavoring. Layer together in a large bowl, starting with strawberries then adding cake mixture. Continue layering; finish with strawberries. Cover with plastic wrap. Chill well.

Yield: 24 servings.

Walter Lehman, Essenhaus Foods

Bundt Cake

1 box yellow cake mix
1 box instant vanilla pudding
3/4 cup vegetable oil
3/4 cup water
3 eggs

1 tsp. vanilla
1 tsp. butter flavoring
1/3 cup sugar
2 tsp. cinnamon
1/3 cup nuts

Mix cake mix, pudding, oil, and water. Add eggs and beat well at high speed for 5 minutes. Add vanilla and butter flavoring.

Grease bundt pan well with margarine. Mix sugar, cinnamon, and nuts. Put half this mixture in bottom of pan, then add half the cake mix. Repeat layers.

Bake 40-50 minutes at 350°.

Mary Esther Miller, waitress

Raspberry Freeze

1/4 cup honey
1 (8 oz.) pkg, cream cheese
1 (10 oz.) pkg. frozen raspberries, partially thawed

1 cup banana slices
2 cups miniature marshmallows
1 cup heavy cream, whipped

Gradually add honey to cream cheese, mixing until well blended. Stir in fruit; fold in marshmallows and whipped cream. Pour into a 9" square pan. Freeze. Place in refrigerator 30 minutes before serving. Makes 9 servings.

Variation: Pour mixture into 10 - 5 oz. paper cups; insert wooden sticks in center. Freeze. Thaw slightly in refrigerator before serving.

Sue Miller, manager

Chocolate Angel Food Cake

Cake:
2 cups egg whites
2 tsp. cream of tartar
2 cups sugar
2 tsp. vanilla
1 cup + 5 tbsp. cake flour
1/2 tsp. salt
3 tbsp. cocoa

Frosting:
1/2 cup margarine
1/4 cup cocoa
1/3 cup buttermilk
1/2 tsp. vanilla
powdered sugar

In a large bowl, beat egg whites and cream of tartar until foamy. Add 1 cup sugar, 2 tbsp. at a time, beating after each addition. When all sugar has been added, beat until stiff. Fold in vanilla. Sift cake flour, sugar, salt, and cocoa. Fold into egg whites. Pour into angel food cake pan. Bake at 375° for 45 to 50 minutes.

For frosting, in a saucepan mix margarine, cocoa, and buttermilk and bring to a boil. Add vanilla and enough powdered sugar to make a spreadable consistency.

Mattie Diener, waitress

Pumpkin Roll

3 eggs
1 cup sugar
2/3 cup pumpkin
1 tsp. lemon juice
3/4 cup flour
1 tsp. baking powder
2 tsp. cinnamon
1 tsp. ginger
1/2 tsp. nutmeg

Filling:
1 cup powdered sugar
8 oz. cream cheese
4 tbsp. margarine
1 tsp. vanilla

Beat eggs; gradually add sugar, pumpkin and lemon juice. Fold in flour; stir in spices. Grease and flour a cookie sheet. Pour batter into pan and bake at 375° for 15 minutes. While cake is still warm, turn out onto a clean towel sprinkled with powdered sugar and roll up cake and towel together, beginning at short end. When cake is cool, unroll and spread with filling.

Beat cream cheese, margarine, and powdered sugar until smooth. Stir in vanilla. Spread on cooled cake. Sprinkle with chopped nuts if desired. Reroll cake, beginning at short end. Freeze, or keep in refrigerator. Slice to serve.

Mary Esther Miller, waitress

Chocolate Zucchini Cake

3 squares unsweetened chocolate
3 cups unsifted flour
1 tsp. baking soda
1 1/2 tsp. baking powder
1 tsp. salt

4 eggs
3 cups sugar
1 1/2 cups oil
3 cups shredded zucchini
1 cup chopped nuts

Melt and cool chocolate. Sift together dry ingredients. Beat eggs until thick and creamy. Add dry ingredients. Stir in sugar, oil, chocolate, zucchini, and nuts.

Bake in a greased 9"x13" pan at 350° for 1 hour and 15 minutes.

Alice Risser, cashier
Dutch Country Gifts

Pretzel Dessert

2 cups coarsely crushed pretzels
3/4 cup melted margarine
3 tsp. sugar
8 oz. cream cheese
1 cup sugar

8 oz. Cool Whip®
6 oz. pkg. strawberry Jello®
2 cups boiling water
2 - 10 oz. pkgs. frozen strawberries.

Mix pretzels, margarine, and 3 tsp. sugar. Press into a 9"x13" pan. Bake at 400° for 8 minutes. Cool.

Combine cream cheese, sugar, and Cool Whip®. Blend well and spread over cooled crust. Refrigerate.

Combine Jello®, boiling water and strawberries. When slightly congealed, pour over the top of cheese mixture. Refrigerate.

*Use blueberry or black raspberry Jello® in place of strawberry.
*Use blueberries or black raspberries in place of strawberries.

Bill Burns, bakery

Cream-Filled Sponge Cake

Cake:
1 box yellow cake mix
1 box instant vanilla pudding
1 cup water
4 eggs
1/2 cup vegetable oil

Filling:
5 tbsp. flour
1 1/4 cups milk
1 cup sugar
1/2 cup butter
1/2 cup shortening
1/2 tsp. salt
1 tsp. vanilla

Mix cake ingredients thoroughly. Pour into 2 greased and floured 9"x13" pans. Bake for 15-20 minutes at 325°.

For filling, combine flour and milk in saucepan and cook, stirring occasionally, until thick. Set aside to cool. Mixture must be cold before adding to other ingredients.

Mix remaining ingredients and beat until fluffy. Add cooked mixture and beat again until fluffy. Spread on 1 cake and place the other cake on top.

Lou Anna Yoder, bakery; Ruth Ann Bontrager, busser

Peanut Delight

1st layer: 2/3 cup chopped peanuts or pecans
1 cup flour
1/2 cup butter

Blend and bake in a 9"x13" pan at 350° for 20 minutes. Cool.

2nd layer: 1/3 cup peanut butter (opt.)
1 (8 oz.) pkg. cream cheese
1 cup powdered sugar
2 cups Cool Whip®

Cream together all of the above. Spread over cooled crust.

3rd layer: 1 box instant vanilla pudding
1 box instant chocolate or pistachio pudding
3 cups milk

Mix until blended. Pour over cream cheese layer.

4th layer: Top with Cool Whip®, 1/3 cup peanuts, and grated Hershey bar.

Edna Bontrager, Mary Miller, Ella Bontrager, Wilma Weaver, Rosie Eash

Creme de Menthe Cake

Cake:
1 box white cake mix
1/3 cup creme de menthe syrup
   or 1/3 cup water

Topping:
1 can Hershey's® Fudge
1 (8 oz.) Cool Whip®
1/4 cup creme de menthe syrup
green food coloring

   Mix cake mix as directed on box, stirring in creme de menthe syrup or water. Bake in a 9"x13" pan according to package directions.
   Spread fudge over cooled cake. Mix Cool Whip®, syrup, and a few drops of food coloring. Spread over fudge. Store cake in the refrigerator.

Malinda Eash, Loom Creations

Peach-A-Berry Cobbler

1 tbsp. cornstarch
1/4 cup brown sugar
1/2 cup cold water
2 cups fresh, sugared, sliced peaches
1 cup fresh blueberries
1 tbsp. butter or margarine
1 tbsp. lemon juice

Crust:
1 cup flour
1/2 cup sugar
1 1/2 tsp. baking powder
1/2 tsp. salt
1/2 cup milk
1/4 cup margarine

Nutmeg Topper:
1/4 tsp. nutmeg   2 tbsp. sugar

Mix first 3 ingredients with fruit. Cook and stir till thick. Add butter and lemon juice. Pour into baking dish.

Sift dry crust ingredients; add milk and butter at once. Beat till smooth. Spread over fruit. Mix topping ingredients; sprinkle over crust.

Bake at 350° for 30 minutes. Serve with milk.

LaVerda Miller, waitress

Crumb Cake

2 1/2 cups flour
3/4 tsp. salt
1 1/2 cups brown sugar
1/2 cup shortening
1 tsp. baking soda

1 cup sour milk
1/2 tsp. cinnamon
1/2 tsp. cloves
1 tsp. vanilla

Mix flour, salt, and brown sugar. Cut in shortening until mixture is crumbly. Save 1 cup crumbs for top. Mix the baking soda and sour milk; add to remaining crumbs. Stir in vanilla and spices. Pour into a 9"x9" pan. Sprinkle with reserved 1 cup crumbs.

Bake in a 350° oven for 25-30 minutes.

Katie Miller, gift shop

Old Fashioned Apple Dumplings

6 medium-sized baking apples
2 cups flour
2 1/2 tsp. baking powder
1/2 tsp. salt
2/3 cup shortening
1/2 cup milk
sugar & cinnamon

Sauce:
2 cups brown sugar
2 cups water
1/4 cup butter
1/4 tsp. cinnamon or nutmeg

Pare and core apples. Cut in halves. To make pastry, sift flour, baking powder and salt together. Cut in shortening until particles are about the size of small peas. Sprinkle milk over mixture and press together lightly, working dough only enough to hold together. Roll dough as for pastry and cut into 12 squares. Place half an apple on each. Fill cavity in apple with sugar and cinnamon. Pat dough around apple to cover it completely. Fasten edges securely on top of apple. Place dumplings 1" apart in a greased baking pan.

Pour sauce over. Combine brown sugar, water and spices. Cook for 5 minutes, remove from heat, and add butter. Bake at 375° for 35-40 minutes. Baste occasionally during baking. Serve hot with half & half or ice cream.

Delicious Coffee Cake

Cake:
2 cups flour
1 cup sugar
1 tsp. salt
4 eggs
1 cup oil
1 can fruit pie filling

Topping:
1/2 cup brown sugar
1 tbsp. margarine
1/2 tsp. cinnamon
chopped nuts (opt.)

Glaze:
1 cup powdered sugar
milk

Mix all cake ingredients except pie filling. Pour half of the batter into a greased 9"x13" cake pan. Cover with pie filling. Pour in remaining batter. Mix topping ingredients and sprinkle over cake.

Bake at 350° for 30 minutes. Cool. For glaze, mix powdered sugar with enough milk to make runny. Drizzle over cake.

Ellen Mishler, hostess/cashier

Individual Cheesecakes

18 vanilla wafers
1/2 cup sugar
2 tsp. vanilla
2 eggs

2 pkgs. (8 oz. each) cream cheese
1 can (22 oz.) cherry or blueberry pie filling

Place 18 paper cupcake liners in muffin tins. Put 1 vanilla wafer in each. Mix eggs, sugar, cream cheese, and vanilla together at medium speed for 5 minutes. Spoon into liners until each is 3/4 full.

Bake at 375° for 12-15 minutes. Let cool, then spoon on pie filling. Serves 18.

Lynette Zimmerman, grill worker

Delicious Raspberry Cake

1 regular-size box white cake mix
2/3 cup vegetable oil
4 eggs

1 (3 oz.) box raspberry jello
1 (10 oz.) pkg. frozen red raspberries, thawed (also use juice)

Mix all ingredients together. Bake in a 9"x13" pan at 325° for 50 minutes.

Katie Miller, Dutch Country Gifts

Our talk ain't so for fanciness
But plain, it makes just right.
It ain't so good dressed up in print,
But from the heart it comes out bright.

Homemade Ice Cream

6 eggs
2 1/2 cups sugar
pinch salt

1 can sweetened condensed milk
1 quart whipping cream
3 tbsp. vanilla

Beat eggs with electric mixer until well blended. Add sugar and salt slowly. Continue to mix and add sweetened condensed milk, whipping cream, and vanilla. Pour contents into freezer can and add whole milk to fill line. Be sure to stir well before freezing. Freeze immediately.

Makes 1 1/2 gallons.

Glenda Yoder, waitress
Pamela Frey, bakery

Easy Carrot Cake

1 yellow cake mix
1 1/4 cups Miracle Whip®
4 eggs
1/4 cup cold water
2 tsp. cinnamon

2 cups shredded carrots
1/2 cup chopped walnuts
cream cheese ready-to-spread
   frosting

Mix cake mix, Miracle Whip®, eggs, water, and cinnamon. Mix until blended. Stir in carrots and walnuts. Spread in a 9"x13" baking pan.
Bake at 350° for 35 minutes. Cool. Spread with cream cheese frosting.

Sharon Boley, waitress

Swallow your pride occasionally. It's not fattening.

Heath Bar Delight

1 pkg. Lorna Doone® cookies, crumbled
1 stick melted butter or margarine
2 pkgs. instant vanilla pudding
2 cups milk
1 qt. softened Heath® bar ice cream (other flavors may be substituted)
8 oz. Cool Whip®
6 Heath® bars, crushed

Mix cookie crumbs and melted butter. Press into the bottom of a 9"x13" dish.

Mix pudding, milk, and ice cream and pour over crumb mixture. Refrigerate 6 hours or overnight. Top with Cool Whip and sprinkle with crushed Heath bars.

Edna Mae Schmucker, dishwasher

Fresh Apple Cake

1/2 cup shortening or oil
2 cups sugar
2 eggs
2 cups flour
2 tsp. baking soda
1/2 - 1 tsp. salt

2 tsp. cinnamon
1/2 tsp. nutmeg
4 cups chopped apples
1 cup nuts
1/2 - 1 cup cooked raisins

Cream shortening; add sugar and beat until fluffy. Add eggs; beat. Combine all dry ingredients and add to egg mixture. Stir in apples, nuts, and raisins. Pour into a greased 9"x13" pan.

Bake 45 minutes at 350°.

Olive Bontrager, cashier

Grandma Clark's Rice Pudding

1 cup rice
1 tbsp. margarine
2 cups water
1 tsp. salt

1 egg
1 cup milk
1 tsp. vanilla
1/2 cup raisins

Mix rice, margarine, water, and salt and bring to a boil. Cook 14 minutes. Let sit until dry-looking.

Beat the egg and milk and add to rice mixture. Stir in vanilla and raisins. Cook over low heat until thickened. Put in serving dish. Brown 2 to 3 tsp. butter. Sprinkle brown sugar over rice and pour butter over.

Bill Burns, bakery

Happy Valley Chocolate Cake

3 cups flour
2 cups white sugar
2 tsp. baking soda
6 tbsp. cocoa
1 tsp. salt

2 cups cold water
2 tsp. vanilla
2 tsp. vinegar
1/2 cup + 2 tbsp. vegetable oil

Mix dry ingredients; add remaining ingredients. Bake in a 9"x13" pan at 375° for 35 minutes, or until toothpick comes out clean.

Katie Miller, gift shop

If you don't want your children to hear what you're saying, pretend you're talking to them.

Fruit Pizza

1 tube refrigerated sugar cookie dough
8 oz. cream cheese, softened
12 oz. Cool Whip®

fruits: pineapple chunks, banana slices, strawberries, sliced peaches, mandarin oranges, cherries, blueberries, kiwi

Thinly slice sugar cookie dough and press onto a pizza pan. Bake 10-12 minutes at 350°. Cool.

Mix cream cheese and Cool Whip®. (If it's too stiff add a little pineapple juice to make it creamy.) Spread on top of cookie dough. Arrange fruits of choice on top of cream cheese. Chill.

Rosalie Bontrager, manager, Essenhaus Country Inn

Hot Fudge Sundae Cake

1 cup flour
2 tsp. cocoa
1/4 tsp. salt
2 tsp. vegetable oil
1 cup nuts
3/4 cup sugar
2 tsp. baking powder
1/2 cup milk
1 tsp. vanilla
1 cup brown sugar
1/4 cup cocoa
1 1/3 cups hot water

Mix flour, cocoa, salt, oil, nuts, sugar, baking powder, milk, and vanilla. Pour into a greased baking pan. Sprinkle brown sugar and 1/4 cup cocoa over batter. Then pour the hot water over batter. Do not stir; this makes the sauce.

Bake 40 minutes at 350°. Delicious with ice cream.

Lizzie Ann Bontrager, cook

Frozen Mocha Cheesecake

1 1/4 cups chocolate wafer cookie crumbs (about 24 cookies)
1/4 cup sugar
1/4 cup butter or margarine, melted
1 (8 oz.) pkg. cream cheese, softened
1 (14 oz.) can sweetened condensed milk
2/3 cup chocolate syrup
2 tbsp. instant coffee
1 tsp. hot water
1 cup whipping cream, whipped

In a small bowl, combine cookie crumbs, sugar, and butter. Pat crumbs into a 9"x13" pan (sides and bottom). Chill.

In a large bowl, beat cream cheese until fluffy; add sweetened condensed milk and chocolate syrup. In a small bowl, dissolve coffee in hot water and add to cream cheese mixture; mix well. Fold in whipped cream. Pour into prepared pan; cover.

Freeze for 6 hours or until firm. Garnish with additional chocolate crumbs if desired. Return leftovers to freezer.

Katie Miller, Dutch Country Gifts

Oatmeal Chocolate Chip Cake

1 3/4 cups boiling water
1 cup uncooked oatmeal (quick or regular)
1 cup lightly packed brown sugar
1 cup white sugar
1/2 cup butter
2 extra large eggs
1 3/4 cups unsifted flour
1/2 tsp. salt
1 tsp. baking soda
1 heaping tbsp. cocoa
1 pkg. (12. oz.) chocolate chips
3/4 cup walnuts

In large bowl, pour boiling water over oatmeal. Let stand for 10 minutes. Add brown sugar, white sugar, and butter. Stir till butter melts. Add eggs; mix well. Add dry ingredients; mix well. Add 1/2 package chocolate chips, mix, and pour into greased 9"x13" pan. Top with nuts and rest of chocolate chips.

Bake at 350° for 40-45 minutes.

Beth Ann Yoder

Death By Chocolate

1 - 9"x13" pan of brownies, baked, cooled, crumbled, and divided in half
2 pkgs. chocolate mousse mix, prepared as package directs and divided
16 oz. Cool Whip®
8 chocolate-toffee bars - regular size, crushed and divided
1 cup pecans, divided

Layer half of each ingredient in a large bowl or 9"x13" pan in the order given. Repeat. Cover dessert and refrigerate overnight.

Dick Carpenter, material handling

Prayer should be the key of the day and the lock of the night.

Peach Custard Cake

1 1/2 cups flour
1/2 tsp. salt
1/2 cup butter or margarine, softened
1 lb. 14 oz. can sliced peaches, drained, reserve syrup

1/2 cup sugar
1/2 tsp. cinnamon
1 egg, slightly beaten
1 cup evaporated milk

In a bowl, mix flour, salt, and butter with a pastry blender until mixture looks like coarse meal. With the back of a spoon, press mixture firmly on bottom and halfway up sides of a buttered 8" pan.

Drain peaches well, saving 1/2 cup syrup. Arrange drained peaches on crust in pan. Mix sugar and cinnamon and sprinkle over peaches. Bake at 375° for 20 minutes.

Mix the peach syrup, egg, and evaporated milk. Pour over peaches. Bake for 30 minutes more, or until custard is firm except in center. Center becomes firm on standing. Serve warm or cold.

Millie Yoder, cashier

Dirt Pudding

1 - 12 oz. pkg. Oreo® cookies, crushed
1 - 8 oz. pkg. Cool Whip®
1 - 8 oz. pkg. cream cheese, softened
1 cup powdered sugar
1/2 stick margarine, softened
2 pkg. French vanilla instant pudding
3 1/2 cups milk

Spread crushed cookies on bottom of a 9"x13" pan, reserving 1/2 cup crumbs for later use. Mix whipped topping, cream cheese, powdered sugar, and margarine. In a separate bowl, mix pudding and milk. Mix with cream cheese mixture and spread over the cookies. Top with the 1/2 cup cookie crumbs. Chill well.

Wilma Weaver, waitress

Rhubarb Cake

Cake:
1 1/2 cups rhubarb, finely cut
1/2 cup sugar
2 cups flour
1 1/2 cups sugar
1/2 cup vegetable oil

2 eggs, beaten
1 cup sour milk
1 tsp. baking soda
1 tsp. cinnamon
1 tsp. vanilla

Topping:
6 tbsp. butter or margarine
2/3 cups brown sugar
1 cup nuts
1 cup coconut
1/4 cup milk

Combine rhubarb with 1/2 cup sugar and set aside. Mix flour, 1 1/2 cups sugar, oil, egg, sour milk, soda, cinnamon, and vanilla. Add the rhubarb and sugar mixture. Stir until well blended. Pour into greased and floured 9"x13" pan. Bake at 350° for 1 hour or until done.

Combine topping ingredients in a saucepan and cook 3 minutes. Pour topping over cake while warm.

Katie Cross, waitress

Cinnamon Pudding

1 cup brown sugar
3/4 cup cold water
1 tbsp. butter
2 cups flour
1 cup sugar

2 tsp. baking powder
2 tsp. cinnamon
2 tbsp. butter
1 cup milk
1 cup pecans

In a saucepan, combine brown sugar, water, and butter and bring to a boil. Pour into a 9"x13" pan.

Sift flour, sugar, baking powder, and cinnamon. Add butter and milk; beat well. Pour over first mixture. Add pecans.

Bake at 350° for about 45 minutes. Serve with whipped cream or ice cream.

Karen Lehman, waitress
Betty Graber, waitress

Sour Cream Coffee Cake

1/2 cup butter, softened
1 cup sugar
2 eggs
8 oz. sour cream (1 cup)
1 tsp. vanilla
2 cups all-purpose flour
1 tsp. baking powder
1 tsp. baking soda

1/4 tsp. salt

Topping:
1/3 cup brown sugar
1/4 cup sugar
2 tsp. cinnamon
1/2 cup chopped nuts

Combine topping ingredients and set aside.

Cream butter and sugar in a bowl. Add eggs, sour cream, and vanilla. Mix well. Combine flour, baking powder, baking soda, and salt. Add to butter and egg mixture. Beat until combined.

Pour half the batter into a greased 9"x13" pan. Sprinkle with half the topping mixture. Add remaining batter and then remaining topping. Bake at 325° for 40 minutes, or until done.

Ida Weaver, waitress

Bread pudding

10-12 rolls (day old) or rolls and bread enough to fill a 9"x13" pan
5 cups milk
2 cups sugar
10 eggs, beaten
1 tbsp. vanilla

Lemon Sauce:
1/4 cup lemon juice
1/2 cup sugar
4 cups hot water
pinch salt
cornstarch
yellow food coloring

Cut up rolls and bread and put in pan. Meanwhile, heat the milk. Remove from heat and add the sugar, eggs, and vanilla. Mix and pour over rolls. Sprinkle cinnamon or nutmeg over top and bake, uncovered, at 350° until set and browned. Serve hot pudding with lemon sauce over the top.

Heat lemon juice, sugar, hot water, and salt. Stir in a bit of cornstarch and continue to heat and stir until mixture thickens. Add more cornstarch until desired consistency is reached. Add a few drops yellow food coloring.

Lydia Ann Miller, head cook

Turtle Cake

1 pkg German Chocolate cake mix
1 stick butter (4 oz.)
14 oz. caramels
7 oz. sweetened condensed milk
6 oz. chopped pecans
6 oz. semi-sweet chocolate chips

Mix cake as directed on package. Pour half the batter into a greased and floured 9"x13" pan and bake at 350° for 15 minutes.

In top of double boiler, melt butter, caramels and milk. Remove top of double boiler from heat. Cool mixture slightly and pour over baked half of cake. Pour on remaining cake batter. Sprinkle with pecans and chocolate chips.

Bake at 350° for 25 minutes.

Mary Ann Schlabach, waitress

Baked Rhubarb Crunch

3 cups diced rhubarb
1/2 cup white sugar
1 tbsp. flour
1/2 tsp. nutmeg
1 cup brown sugar

3/4 cup flour
1 cup quick oats
1/2 tsp. salt
3/4 cup butter

In bottom of a greased pan, place thoroughly mixed rhubarb, white sugar, 1 tbsp. flour and nutmeg. Combine brown sugar, remaining flour, oats and salt; cut in butter as you would for pastry, and sprinkle on top of rhubarb mixture.

Bake 30-40 minutes at 375° or until crisp and nicely browned.

Katie Miller, Dutch Country Gifts
Laura Anna Miller, grill

Angel Food Pie

1 1/4 cups sugar
1/4 cup cornstarch
pinch salt
2 cups boiling water
2 egg whites, beaten

1 cup crushed pineapple, drained
1 tsp. vanilla
1 baked pie shell
whipped cream

Sift sugar, cornstarch and salt. Add to boiling water and boil till thick. Pour over beaten egg whites and beat well. Add pineapple and vanilla. Pour into baked pie shell and top with whipped cream.

Lydia Mae Troyer, cook
Martha Otto, pie baker

Short Cut Pastry

2 cups flour
2 tsp. sugar
1 1/4 tsp. salt

3 tbsp. milk
2/3 cup vegetable oil (scant)

Combine flour, sugar, and salt. Add milk and oil. Mix with fork until all flour is moistened. Save about 1/3 cup of dough to top pie. Press remaining dough evenly in pie pan, covering bottom and sides. Crimp the edges. Add fruit filling. Bake as fruit pie recipe directs.

Can be used for pot pie dough too.

Katie Ann Lehman, cook

Blueberry Lemon Pie

2 1/2 cups water
2 cups sugar
1 cup fresh blueberries
3 tbsp. Sure•Jell®
1/2 tsp. salt
1/2 cup water
1/2 cup sugar

3 oz. pkg. lemon jello
4 cups fresh blueberries
1 cup whipping cream
8 oz. cream cheese
1 cup powdered sugar
1 baked pie shell

Mix 2 1/2 cups water, 2 cups sugar, and 1 cup fresh blueberries together in a saucepan and bring to a boil. Mix Sure•Jell, salt, 1/2 cup water, and 1/2 cup sugar together and add to boiling mixture. Cook until clear. Add jello and then cool mixture. Add 4 cups fresh blueberries.

Beat whipped cream. Add cream cheese and powdered sugar. Beat until smooth. Line baked pie shell with cream mixture, saving enough for the top. Add blueberry filling and then top with remaining cream mixture.

Mary Arlene Bontrager, waitress

Never Fail Pie Crust

3 cups flour
1 tsp. salt
1 1/2 cups shortening

1 egg
1 tsp. vinegar
5 tbsp. cold water

Mix flour and salt. Cut in shortening until mixture is crumbly. Beat together egg, vinegar, and water. Add to flour mixture a little at a time, mixing well.

Makes 3 pie crusts.

Betty Miller, pie baker

Before you begin to give someone a piece of your mind, consider carefully whether you can spare any.

Bob Andy Pie

1 cup brown sugar
1 cup white sugar
3 heaping tbsp. flour
1 tsp. cinnamon
1/2 tsp. cloves

1 heaping tbsp. butter
3 eggs, separated
3 cups milk
2 unbaked pie shells

Mix together dry ingredients. Add butter, beaten egg yolks, and milk. Fold in beaten egg whites and pour into pie shells.

Bake at 450° for 10 minutes. Reduce heat to 350° and bake until done, approximately 35 minutes more.

Makes 2 pies.

Katie Miller, gift shop

Velvety Custard Pie

4 eggs, slightly beaten
1/2 cup sugar
1/4 tsp. salt

1 tsp. vanilla
2 1/2 cups milk, scalded
1 - 9" unbaked pie shell

Beat eggs, sugar, salt, and vanilla together. Pour in the hot milk and beat again. Pour into unbaked pie shell. Sprinkle with nutmeg and cinnamon if desired.

Bake in a very hot oven, 475°, for 5 minutes. Reduce heat to 425° and bake 10 minutes more. Cool on rack.

Sharon Boley, waitress

Coconut Cream Pie

2/3 cup sugar
1/2 tsp. salt
2 1/2 tbsp. cornstarch
1 tbsp. flour
3/4 cup coconut
3 cups milk

3 egg yolks
1 tbsp. butter
1 1/2 tsp. vanilla
1 baked pie shell
meringue or Cool Whip®

Mix all ingredients and cook over a medium heat, stirring constantly, until mixture begins to thicken. Pour into baked pie shell. Top with meringue or Cool Whip.

Ruth Ann Wagler, kitchen and bakery

Strawberry Pie

Pie Crust:
1 cup flour
3 tbsp. powdered sugar
1 stick (1/2 cup) margarine

Filling:
1 cup sugar
1 cup water
3 tbsp. cornstarch
3 tbsp. strawberry Jello® (dry)
1 qt. strawberries, halved

For crust, mix flour and powdered sugar; cut in margarine. Pat into pie pan, crimping over the edge slightly. Bake about 10 minutes at 350°; cool.

Combine sugar, water and cornstarch in a saucepan. Cook until thick and clear. Add strawberry Jello® and stir until dissolved.

Fill crust with well-drained, halved strawberries (approximately 1 quart). Pour filling over berries and refrigerate pie until firm.

Mildred Two, cake decorator

Cream Cheese Pecan Pie

8 oz. cream cheese, softened
1/2 cup sugar
1 egg, beaten
1/2 tsp. salt
1 tsp. vanilla
1 (10") unbaked pie shell

1 1/4 cups chopped pecans

Topping:
3 eggs
1/2 tsp. vanilla
1 cup light corn syrup

Cream together softened cream cheese, sugar, beaten egg, salt and vanilla. Spread over bottom of unbaked pie shell. Sprinkle pecans evenly over cream cheese layer.

Combine all topping ingredients and beat till smooth. Pour over pecan layer. Bake for 35-45 minutes at 375° until pecan layer is golden brown. Serve slightly warm with whipped cream if desired.

Yields 12 servings.

Ellen Miller, gift shop cashier

Shoofly Pie

2 cups flour
1 1/2 cups brown sugar
1/4 tsp. salt
4 tbsp. margarine
2 beaten eggs

2 cups molasses
2 cups hot water, divided use
2 tsp. baking soda
2 unbaked pie shells

Mix flour, brown sugar, salt, and margarine till crumbly. Take out 2 cups of crumbs for top of pies.

To remainder of crumbs add eggs, molasses, and 1 1/2 cups hot water. Mix well. Dissolve baking soda in remaining 1/2 cup hot water and add to molasses mixture.

Pour into pie shells and top with reserved crumbs. Place pies on cookie sheet. Bake at 450° for 10 minutes. Reduce heat to 375° and bake for 30 minutes more, or until top is dry and done.

*Instead of molasses you can use 1 1/2 cups dark corn syrup, 1/2 light corn syrup, 2 tsp. vanilla and 1/4 tsp. maple flavoring.

Dutch Apple Pie

3 cups diced apples
1 cup sugar
2 tbsp. half & half
1/2 tsp. cinnamon
1 tbsp. flour
2 tbsp. butter

1 unbaked pie shell

Crumbs:
1/2 cup sugar
1/3 cup butter
3/4 cup flour

Mix together the first six ingredients and put in the pie shell. Mix crumb ingredients together until crumbly and sprinkle over top.

Bake pie at 450° for 45 minutes.

Katie Cross, waitress

What goes into your mind comes out of your mouth.

Rhubarb Custard Pie

2 cups diced rhubarb
3/4 cup sugar
1/4 tsp. salt
2 tbsp. flour

2 egg yolks
1 cup milk
2 tbsp. butter
1 unbaked pie shell

Meringue:
2 egg whites
pinch salt

2 tbsp. powdered sugar

Add sugar, salt, and flour to the slightly beaten egg yolks. Scald the milk and add butter. When butter is melted, pour the milk into the egg mixture and mix thoroughly. Spread rhubarb in pie shell and cover with egg and milk mixture. Bake at 425° for 20 minutes. Reduce heat to 325° and bake 25 minutes.

For meringue, beat egg whites and salt until foamy. Gradually add powdered sugar, beating until peaks form. Spread meringue over hot pie, sealing to edges of pie crust. Return to oven until meringue is golden brown.

Martha Otto, pie baker

Fudge Sundae Pie

1/4 cup corn syrup
2 tbsp. firmly packed brown sugar
3 tbsp. margarine
2 1/2 cups crisp rice cereal
1/4 cup peanut butter

1/4 cup fudge sauce (for ice cream)
3 tbsp. corn syrup
1 quart vanilla ice cream

Combine the 1/4 cup corn syrup, brown sugar, and margarine in a medium-sized saucepan. Cook over low heat, stirring occasionally until mixture begins to boil. Remove from heat and add rice cereal. Stir until well coated. Press evenly into 9" pie pan to form crust.

Stir together peanut butter, fudge sauce, and the 3 tbsp. corn syrup. Spread half the mixture over the crust. Freeze until firm. Allow ice cream to soften slightly. Spoon into frozen crust, spreading evenly. Freeze until firm.

Let pie stand at room temperature about 10 minutes before cutting. Warm remaining peanut butter mixture and drizzle over the top.

Betti Kauffman, cashier/hostess

Raspberry Cream Pie

3/4 cup water
1/2 cup sugar
1 heaping tbsp. Sure•Jell®, or
  1 level tbsp. cornstarch
pinch salt
1/4 cup cold water
1/4 tsp. lemon juice
4 oz. raspberry Jello®
2 cups fresh red raspberries
4 cups cooled vanilla pie filling
2 baked 9" pie crusts
whipped cream

In a saucepan, combine 3/4 cup water and the sugar. Bring to a boil. Meanwhile, mix Sure•Jell®, salt, cold water, and lemon juice. Add to the boiling mixture and continue to boil until mixture is clear. Stir in the raspberry Jello®. Cool, and add fresh raspberries.

Put 2 cups of vanilla pie filling in the bottom of each baked pie crust. Place 1 cup of raspberry mixture on top of the pie filling and top with whipped cream. Makes 2 pies.

Mary Esther Miller, bakery

Fruit Pie with 7-Up®

1 1/2 cups 7-Up®
1 cup sugar
2 tbsp. Sure•Jell®

1 box Jello® to match fruit
choice of fruit
1 baked pie shell

Boil first 3 ingredients together. Add Jello®. When about set, add fruit. Pour into baked pie shell and top with whipped cream.

Wilma Schlabach, dessert counter

Thou shalt the Sabbath not misuse, nor come to church to take thy snooze.

Peanut Butter Pie

1/2 cup white sugar
1/2 cup brown sugar
2/3 cup flour
3 eggs, beaten
1/4 tsp. salt
4 cups milk, divided use
1/4 tsp. vanilla

2 tbsp. butter
2 baked pie shells
whipped cream for topping

Crumbs:
1 1/2 cups powdered sugar
2/3 cup peanut butter

Mix sugars, flour, eggs, salt, 3/4 cup cold milk, vanilla, and butter. Scald 3 1/4 cups milk and stir in egg mixture. Continue to heat and stir constantly until thick. Remove from heat and cool.

Mix powdered sugar and peanut butter to form small crumbs. Line each pie shell with crumbs, reserving a few crumbs for topping, and pour in half the pudding. Top with whipped cream and sprinkle reserved crumbs on top. Makes 2 pies.

Ella Bontrager, cook

Green Tomato Pie

3 cups sliced green tomatoes
1/4 tsp. salt
3 tbsp. vinegar
1 1/2 cups sugar
3 tbsp. flour

pastry for 2-crust pie
3 tbsp. butter
1 tsp. cinnamon

Stir tomatoes, salt, vinegar, sugar, and flour together in a bowl and put in an unbaked pie shell. Dot with butter and sprinkle with cinnamon. Put on top crust.

Bake at 400° for 20 minutes. Turn down heat to 350° and bake until brown.

Gayle Martin, bakery

Peach Cream Pie

1 - 9" unbaked pie shell
4-5 large fresh peaches, sliced
1 egg
1 cup sugar

1/4 cup flour
1/2 tsp. vanilla
1 cup cream

Spread peach slices over the bottom of unbaked pie shell. Beat egg. Add sugar and flour. Beat and blend in vanilla and cream. Pour over peaches and sprinkle with cinnamon, if desired. Bake 10 minutes at 400°, and then 350° until done.

Katie Miller, bakery

Lemon Cake Pie

1 cup sugar
pinch salt
2 egg yolks
2 tbsp. melted margarine
2 heaping tbsp. flour

grated rind of 1 large or 2 small lemons
1 cup whole milk
2 egg whites, stiffly beaten
1 unbaked pie shell

Beat sugar, salt, egg yolks, melted margarine, and flour until creamy. Add grated lemon rind. Stir in milk and beaten egg whites. Pour into pie shell.

Bake for 30 minutes in a slow oven at 325°.

Mary K. Schmucker, kitchen
Karen Hochstedler, bakery

Paradise Pumpkin Pie

1 (8 oz.) pkg. cream cheese
1/4 cup sugar
1/2 tsp. vanilla
1 egg
1 - 9" unbaked pastry shell
1 1/4 cups canned pumpkin
1 cup evaporated milk

1/2 cup sugar
2 eggs, slightly beaten
dash salt
1 tsp. cinnamon
1/4 tsp. ginger
1/4 tsp. nutmeg
maple syrup

Combine softened cream cheese, 1/4 cup sugar, and vanilla, mixing until well blended. Add egg; mix well. Spread onto bottom of pastry shell.

Combine remaining ingredients except syrup; mix well. Carefully pour over cream cheese mixture. Bake at 350° for 1 hour and 5 minutes. Cool. Brush with syrup.

Sue Miller, manager

ORDER FORM

Name _____

Address _____

City _____ St. _____ ZIP Code _____

Qty	Title	Price Ea.	Total
	Salads & Appetizers Recipe Sampler	5.99	
	Breads & Soups Recipe Sampler	5.99	
	Salads & Vegetables Recipe Sampler	5.99	
	Main Dishes Recipe Sampler	5.99	
	Cookies Recipe Sampler	5.99	
	Desserts Recipe Sampler	5.99	
	Amish-Country Cookbook - Volume I	12.99	
	Amish-Country Cookbook - Volume II	12.99	
	Amish-Country Cookbook - Volume III	12.99	
		SUBTOTAL	
		Indiana Residents add 5% tax	
		Postage & Handling (10% of Subtotal; $1.50 minimum)	
		TOTAL	

Please see the other side of this form for Payment and Mailing Information.

PAYMENT INFORMATION

☐ **Check/Money Order Enclosed**
Make check or money order payable to "Evangel Publishing House"

☐ **VISA**   ☐ **MasterCard**

Card No. _____ / _____ / _____ / _____

Expiration Date: _____ / _____

Name (as it appears on card): _____

Card holder's signature: _____

Mail this order form and your payment (in U.S. funds) to:
Evangel Publishing House
P.O. Box 189
Nappanee, IN 46550

*Visit our website: www.evangelpublishing.com
or use our toll-free Order Line: 1-800-253-9315 (between 8:00 a.m.-4:30 p.m. EST)*